I0426642

VENOMOUS SNAKES
OF THE SOUTHEAST

II

VENOMOUS SNAKES
OF THE SOUTHEAST

*An Introduction To The
Venomous Snakes Of The
Southeastern United States*

Chad Minter

Contributing Editors:

Karl H. Betz, Derek Egolf, Zack Egolf,
Greg Longhurst, Rich Rumple, B.W. Smith

Published 2005
SeaRay Books

ISBN 1-4116-1779-7
Library of Congress Control Number: 2004099799

This book is dedicated to my parents for putting up with
me when I would drag home every scaly, slimy, crawly,
furred and feathered creature I could get my
hands on when I was growing up;

To my friends who spent countless hours with me trudging
through swamps, fields, and forests in search of
venomous snakes;

And to the snakes themselves for providing me
with so much wonderment.

Acknowledgements

Without the following people's help and friendship, this book would not be possible: Derek Egolf, Zack Egolf, Rich Rumple, Brad Kalota, Chris Harper, Karl H. & Cyndi Betz, Michael Knight, Mardi Snipes, James Dean, Johnny Hester, Carl Adams, B.W. Smith, Daniel Duff, Matt King, Austin Meadows, Glenn Purvis, Marcus Devaney, Tanith Tyrr, Matt O'Connell, Chuck Snow, Delton Hilliard, Jason Barron, Dr. Bob Herrington, Tyler Lee, Chance Gwaltney, Jake Kable, Raviv Gal, Dr. Dennis Parmley, John Hollister, Greg Longhurst and many others...

Disclaimer: This book is intended as an introductory guide to the venomous snakes native to the Southeastern United States. It is not a medical manual. A venomous snakebite can be dangerous to life and limb, and is a serious medical emergency requiring the knowledge and ability of a licensed physician. Never pick up a snake unless you are 100% sure of its identity, and know for certain that it is not dangerous. Snakes are sometimes found outside their normal range.

Venomous snakes should only be handled by people with professional training, experience, and proper tools. Nothing in this book can guarantee your safety when you are in the proximity of a dangerous animal.

The two most important things I can say to you about snakes are:
• **If you see a snake, the safest thing to do is to leave it alone.**
• **If you are bitten by a snake, get immediate medical attention from a licensed and experienced physician.**

Foreword

The ability to write intelligently about a topic means either that the writer has spent a vast number of hours utilizing tedious research techniques, or that the writer has lived his topic. Chad Minter has done both!

The benefit of listening to Chad present his discoveries has been mine many times over. It is an experience to never grow tired of. The sincerity and fire he displays can only come from a true love of his life's passion. It is a love that many cannot understand. For these individual's, he is simply crazy.

Chad's love is specifically snakes. Now you understand the comments previously written.

The majority of Americans fear snakes. In fact, many utterly despise them. Most will relate nightmares of either being chased by snakes or falling into a den of these slinking, slithering, evil creatures. A few will moronically brag on how many or how big the snakes were that they killed. There are even those that cringe and squirm at the thought of watching television programs whose purpose is to educate.

However, for many, there is an unexplainable, eerie fascination in observing these animals. Reptile houses at zoos and carnivals are never lacking of a viewing public. Several television personalities have made careers and became household names by indulging themselves in sensationalistic efforts to amuse and educate. Yet, the standard comment heard from most viewers as the program ends is, "He's crazy!"

Chad is not a sensationalist. He does not have nor want a television program. Instead, Chad simply has a tremendous desire to educate the public about these creatures. That desire comes from his love of the animals and his strong opinions concerning conservation for all creatures.

Our herping expeditions, or "snake hunts" as many would call them, have always been enjoyable and educating. Oh, did I leave out the most important … "safe." The title of "risk taker" is better suited for those that have egos to sate and money to spend on intensive care stays after having been bitten. Safety is always in the forefront of Chad's actions, whether dealing with his personal collection or in the field. The information this publication contains is presented with safety in mind.

Chad's studies have provided a vast kingdom of knowledge from which many can benefit. It is from this reservoir he draws the information for this publication. Yet, he doesn't try to overwhelm you with needless technical information as many do. Chad simply wishes to share basic knowledge with the common person. In doing so, the fear that breeds itself from ignorance can depart, allowing knowledge to assist common sense in conserving these mesmerizing animals and the habitat in which they reside.

So, read what the crazy man has written! It's informative, easy to understand, and filled with tidbits you'll enjoy. There are no hidden serpents lurking in the following pages. Instead, a goldmine of information to keep you safe from venomous reptiles, and to keep them safe from you!

Rich Rumple

Naturalist

The Venomous Snakes of the Southeast United States
A Visual Key

 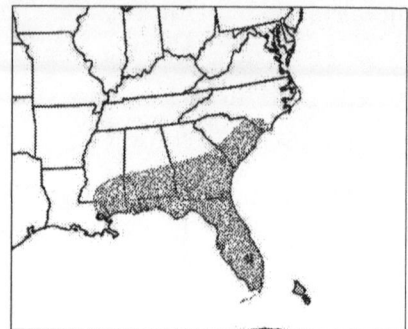

Photo by Chad Minter

Eastern Diamondback Rattlesnake
Crotalus adamanteus

 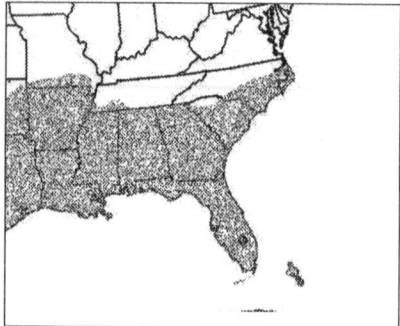

Photo by Chad Minter

Pigmy Rattlesnake
Sistrurus miliarius

 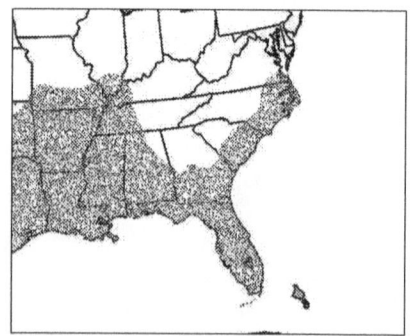

Photo by Chad Minter

Cottonmouth
Agkistrodon piscivorus

The six species of venomous snakes native to the Southeastern United States.
Range maps are approximations, and sometimes snakes are found outside their normal range.

The Venomous Snakes of the Southeast United States
A Visual Key

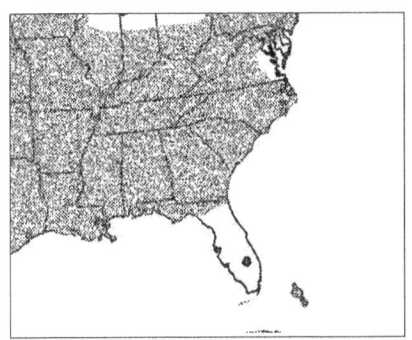 

Photo by Chad Minter

Timber/Canebrake Rattlesnake
Crotalus horridus

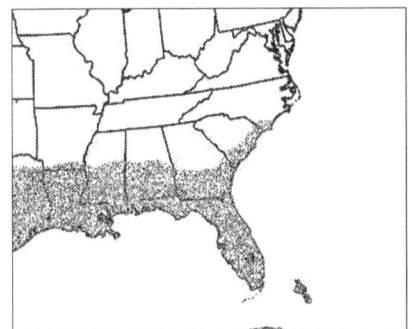 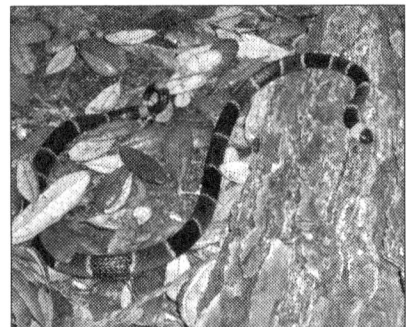

Photo by Zack Egolf

Eastern Coral Snake
Micrurus fulvius

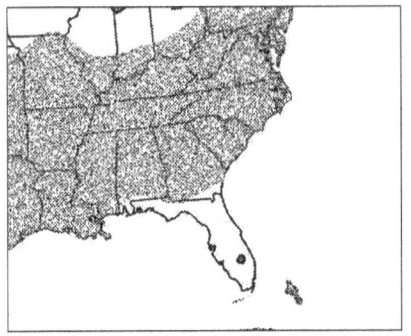 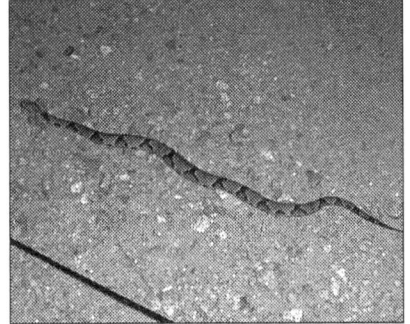

Photo by Chad Minter

Copperhead
Agkistrodon contortrix

The six species of venomous snakes native to the Southeastern United States.
Range maps are approximations, and sometimes snakes are found outside their normal range.

Beneath a tobacco leaf in Vidalia, Georgia, lies a spring coiled and venom loaded surprise. The small green Anolis lizard climbing the stalk in search of insects is unaware that he too is being watched. With each step the lizard takes, he surveys his surroundings carefully. Did something just move? He checks again. No, the coast is clear. Another step, a blinding flash, searing hot pain. Two fangs impaled into his torso, a more than lethal dose of venom, and just a glimpse of the pigmy rattlesnake before his world fades.

Chad Minter

Introduction

Venomous snakes are the most highly developed group of snakes. They are certainly the most intelligent group of snakes. They have an awareness and understanding of their surroundings that non-venomous snakes just do not have. Their ability to kill with a single kiss has attracted the attention of thrill-seekers, scientists, movie-makers, writers, photographers, and religious zealots.

Often in the world of snakes, facts can be as amazing as fiction. Snakes can swallow animals two or three times the size of their own head, go months without food in certain conditions, and they can sit in one spot, waiting patiently for prey to wander by, for as much as seven days, without so much as a twitch. Their camouflage is amazing and can render them virtually invisible, even when only inches away from predator, prey, or herpetologist.

Guiness Book of Worlds Records lists the following records: the oldest snake as 40 years, 3 months, and 14 days old; the longest venomous snake as an 18' 2" King Cobra; the snake with the longest fangs as the Gaboon Viper in Africa; the heaviest living snake as a python weighing 403 pounds; and the most cobras kissed consecutively as 11 monocle cobras and 1 King Cobra by Gordon Cates of Alachua, Florida.

Photo by Chad Minter
All six venomous species in the Southeast U.S. take advantage of Palmetto thickets as cover.

Many questions remain to be answered about snakes. How or why did Rattlesnakes evolve a warning mechanism using sound, when they do not have external ears and cannot hear most sounds? Did Coral Snakes and Kingsnakes develop similar color patterns through parallel evolution or was it mimicry? Is Rattlesnake venom evolving to become more neurotoxic -- and if so, why?

It would seem to make sense that snakes are more primitive than lizards. This is not the case. Snakes evolved from legged reptiles rather than the other way around. Some primitive snakes, such as boas and pythons, still have vestigal limbs and pelvic girdles. The loss of limbs allowed the snakes to go more places in search of prey. Snakes are perfectly suited for retreiving rodents from underground tunnels. They can climb with ease, travel as fast as 12 miles per hour, swim for miles with no problem, and some, such as the Golden Tree Snake, *Chrysopelea ornata*, even glide through the air. Snakes are found in almost every place on earth, from the depths of the world's oceans to the cold and frigid mountains of Russia.

Venomous snakes are dangerous and deadly animals. They should be given a wide berth. Great White Sharks, Grizzly Bears, Eastern Diamondback Rattlesnakes -- It's all the same; Dead is dead. They are beautiful and mysterious animals, environmentally beneficial, medically useful, alluring and interesting, but they are very dangerous animals. Snakes rarely ever 'attack' though they are well prepared to defend themselves. Leave them alone, unless you have been professionally trained to handle them and are willing to take that risk, they can kill you!

"I always keep a flagon of whiskey handy in case I see a snake -- which I also keep handy." --W. C. Fields (1880 - 1946)

"A snake lurks in the grass." --Virgil (70 BC - 19 BC)

"There is no way to catch a snake that is as safe as not catching him."
--Jacob M. Broude

Venomous or Not?

This information is limited to snakes native to the Southeastern United States. It may not apply to species native to other areas.

How does one tell if a snake is venomous?

The easiest way to identify the six species of venomous snakes that are native to the Southeastern U.S. is to use the back cover of this book as a visual reference. A photographic key with a range map for each species is also included on pages XII and XIII.

Only two types of snakes in the Southeastern U.S. are venomous. These are the Pit Vipers and the Coral Snake.

Pit Vipers include Rattlesnakes, the Cottonmouth and the Copperhead. Pit Vipers are heavy bodied snakes with large, triangular heads. Their eyes have elliptical pupils. They have a loreal pit between the eye and nostril that is used to sense heat.

The head of a Pit Viper is triangular because a venom gland is situated above and behind the eye. Venom is delivered to a pair of large hollow, moveable, fangs located in the front of the upper jaw.

The subcaudal scutes (scales) posterior to the vent in a Pit Viper are undivided, while the subcaudal scutes past the vent in Southeastern

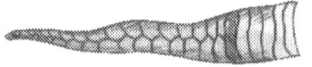

Colubrid (non-venomous) tails have divided subcaudal scutes past the vent on the underside.

Pit Vipers, and Coral Snakes (venomous) have subcaudal scutes that are not divided past the vent on the underside.

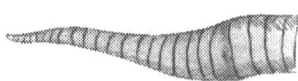

4

Photo by Chad Minter
A Mole Kingsnake. This species is often mistaken for the Copperhead. It is totally harmless.

native non-venomous snakes are divided. (*See Illustration.*)

Simply looking at the pupils of the eye, or at the shape of the head, is <u>not</u> an effective method of telling whether a snake is venomous. The Eastern Diamondback Rattlesnake's eyes and pupils are both black; their eye looks like one big black marble. Many non-venomous snakes also have triangular heads.

The Eastern Coral Snake is a **colorful red, yellow, and black snake <u>with a black nose</u>**. Coral snakes are members of the Elapid family and have a pair of short, fixed front fangs and <u>lack</u> a triangular shaped head.

Some non-venomous snakes have color patterns similar to the Eastern Coral Snake. Examples are the Scarlet Snake and Scarlet Kingsnake, which have <u>red noses</u>. *If you see a snake that is native to the Southeastern U.S., and it is a Pit Viper or a Coral Snake, then it is venomous.*

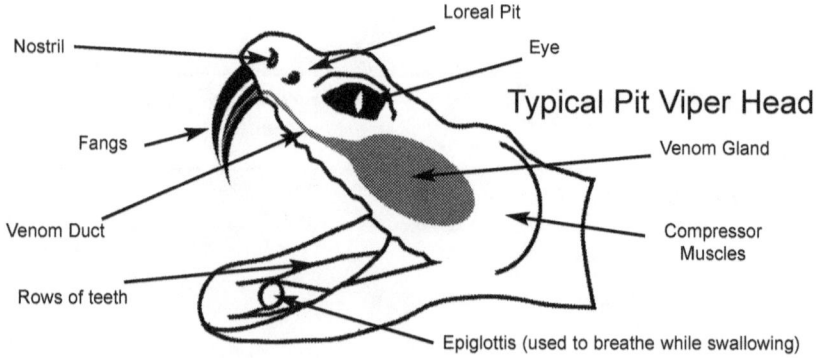

Loreal Pit
Nostril
Eye
Typical Pit Viper Head
Fangs
Venom Gland
Venom Duct
Compressor Muscles
Rows of teeth
Epiglottis (used to breathe while swallowing)

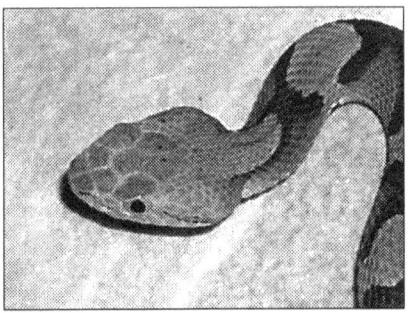 

Photo by Derek Egolf

A copperhead (Agkistrodon contortrix) is a prime example of a pit viper. Notice the two small dots on the parietal scales. These are present in all Southeastern native pit vipers, though they may be hard to see on the dark head of a cottonmouth.

Photo by Matt O'Connell

A black racer (coluber constrictor) has a typical colubrid head. They lack the venom glands behind the eye, and the head is not as dilinieated from the neck as in the pit vipers.

Conservation

Photo by Chad Minter

Snake hunting can be fun! Cottonmouths abound in the creek pictured above. Simply watching where you step can mean the difference between being bitten and not. Notice the lack of Cottonmouths attacking this young man?

Reasons to let snakes live.

In many cases snakes are protected by law. In Georgia, for example, all non-venomous snakes are protected. It is a crime there to kill a water snake, even if you think it is a cottonmouth. Eastern Indigo snakes are federally endangered snakes. They are native to several states across the Southeastern U.S. It is a federal crime to kill or even touch an Eastern Indigo Snake, even if you think it is a venomous snake.

Snakes are beneficial to the environment. They control rodent populations, and as some south-

A Gopher Tortoise crosses a dirt road in South Georgia. This species digs burrows which are used as shelter by a number of species, including the Eastern Diamondback Rattlesnake.

east asian countries have found -- the absence of snakes can cause explosive growth in rodent populations and damage to crops.

Commercial collection of rattlesnakes for 'Rattlesnake Roundups' detrimentally affects the ecosystem. In many cases gasoline is used to drive rattlesnakes from Gopher Tortoise burrows. This kills both Gopher Tortoises and Eastern Indigo Snakes, both of which are endangered species. Gopher tortoise burrows are regularly utilized by many species ranging from insects to foxes. Gassing of these burrows renders them useless for decades.

Venom collected from Rattlesnake Roundups is useless because it is not harvested in sterile laboratory conditions, it is polluted with high levels of endorphins released when the snakes are stressed, and it is not freeze-dried within a time that would prevent the venom from oxidizing and degrading.

Snakes are collected, kept for months without food or water, and literally tortured until dead at these macabre events.

Why isn't there much more of a public outcry against these events?

The absence of predators in the food chain can have catastrophic effects. Mouse and rat populations would explode leaving crops decimated. Disease would flourish, being spread by the mice and rats.

Habitat loss is the single largest threat to wildlife today. Large retail chain stores can pave over 30 acres of Tortoise burrows to build a new store, killing innumerable animals, then abandon the store in a few years leaving the breeding grounds permanently destroyed. It is a FEDERAL CRIME to possess a pair of Gopher Tortises for captive breeding, yet habitat destruction is virtually ignored.

Each acre of land can only support a given number of animals. Every year more habitat is lost to needless development. Old growth forests in the Southeast are clear-cut and replanted with fast growing pine for pulp lumber.

The single most dangerous animal on the face of the earth is the human. No other species has to destroy 3 acres of habitat so that its dwelling can sit in the center of a manicured lawn devoid of creatures.

No other species has a need to shoot, poison, trap, remove, and molest every creature that is unlucky enough to cross its path.

We wonder what happened to all the frogs that we played with as children after warm spring rains, while we sit on our front porches and

Photo by Chad Minter

Photographing venomous snakes should be done carefully and at a safe distance. Notice how James keeps the drum between himself and the coiled Eastern Diamondback Rattlesnake.

Photo by Chad Minter

Don't kill snakes! For every non-venomous snake in an area - that is one venomous snake that you do not have. Any given area can only support a fixed number of snakes. This Eastern Kingsnake even eats venomous snakes. This is a great snake to have around!

watch the trucks go by spraying for mosquitoes. We spray ourselves and our yards with pesticides and weed killers. We dump toxic water into our rivers and streams and complain when the fish are too poisoned to eat. Not-so-brilliant politicians propose saving our national forests from forest fires by cutting down the trees. *Without trees the forests can't catch fire - a brilliant strategy!*

This may be a new concept to some, but guess what -- Mother Nature does NOT need our help. She took care of the universe for millions of eons before we appeared, and she will take care of it for millions of eons after our departure. If we really want to conserve what we have, we should leave it alone!

Brake for Snakes!

Photo by Chad Minter

A neonate Canebrake Rattlesnake (Crotalus horridus atricaudatus) crosses a road on a lazy afternoon in Central Georgia.

We are only guests on this planet, visitors, temporary renters.

Native americans were one of the few cultures that lived in harmony with their environment. They only took what they needed to survive, and nothing more. Why can't we do that?

One thing that has inadvertantly helped the venomous species in the Southeastern U.S. is the introduction of a feral non-native species -- The Fire Ant.

Most venomous snakes in the Southeast bear live young. Most non-venomous snakes in the Southeast are egg layers. Fire ants destroy the eggs of the non-venomous species, lowering their population. Live-bearing venomous snakes move in to exploit the niche previously utilized by the nonvenomous snakes.

Another threat that is decimating populations of all kinds of wildlife is our road system. Many times more snakes die by vehicle than are killed by apathetic individuals with shovels. Would it be that difficult to design roads that funnel wildlife to under-the-road pass-throughs?

There are many problems with today's attempts at conservation. Scientists and Legislators need to take a long hard look at the laws that are on the books, and re-think strategies to conserve wildlife.

Photo by Chad Minter

Mardi Snipes, of Coastal Reptiles, takes a moment to photograph an Eastern Box Turtle crossing a dirt road in Georgia.

Many laws, policies, regulations, and strategies that are in place today actually do more to inhibit conservation than to help. Thousands of Yacare Caimans died after a river was diverted in South America for a hydroelectric plant. Local governments paid people to club the starving and dehydrated animals to death. The U.S. elevated the Yacare Caiman to Cites II. This banned the import of the caimans for the pet trade, and the import of skins for leather. This virtually eliminated any attempts at captive breeding programs. What good does it do to eliminate captive breeding programs, and devalue the animals commercially, when thousands lie dead and rotting in the wild? If the possession of these animals and their parts were legal, then there would be a market for their skins. South Americans would have a reason to farm the caimans and protect the habitat. The animals could then make a comeback.

In many cases commercial collection has helped a species. The corn snake was commercially collected for the pet trade for years. Many people began captive breeding corn snakes. Corn snakes are now available in a myriad of different color and pattern variations as captive bred, healthy, animals. This has virtually eliminated the need for wild caught specimens. Collectors have no need for wild caught corn snakes. They buy captive bred ones. Captive breeding projects reduce pressure on wild popula-

Photo by Chad Minter

Harmless snakes, such as this hognose snake, often flatten their heads out and puff up their bodies to look like a venomous snake.

"She never begins an attack, nor, when once engaged, ever surrenders: She is therefore an emblem of magnanimity and true courage. ... she never wounds 'till she has generously given notice, even to her enemy, and cautioned him against the danger of treading on her."

Benjamin Franklin
Speaking of the Timber Rattlesnake
The National Symbol of the 13 Colonies

tions, simple enough. Why is it that the first piece of legislation to pass to "protect a species" is to ban its possession by the people who would breed them?

There are many examples of captive breeding projects saving a species from extinction.

Pere David's Deer existed only in captive breeding programs. They were hunted to extinction in the wild. In the late 1980's a number of deer were re-introduced into the wild, and have successfully reproduced.

One species of wood duck alive today exists only because of a single clutch of eggs that were found and raised by Gerald Durrell in the U.K. Every duck of this species alive is descended from that one clutch of eggs. What if it had been illegal to collect those eggs, and Mr. Durrell had just walked by because he didn't want to break the law?

Barbary Lions were thought to be extinct for years, until a small colony of them was discovered alive and well in a private zoo.

Australia paid a bounty for every Tasmanian Tiger killed in the early part of this century. The animal was soon totally extinct, with the last animals allegedly gone in the 1930's. Today, cryptozoologists search desperately for just one pair of these animals that might have survived in the

Photo by Chad Minter

A Blackwater Swamp in South Georgia. The water is acidic and has a reddish tint from the presence of tannic acid. Snakes are common in this type of habitat.

remote outback or in a private menagerie. Can't we learn from Australia's mistake and stop paying a bounty on rattlesnakes at rattlesnake roundups? Will our grandchildren wish that we had spared just one pair for a captive breeding program?

Captive breeding programs and private ownership can save species and should be encouraged. Habitat destruction, road-kills and indiscriminate killing should be stopped.

If we are to keep what we have we must respect it. We must leave it alone. We must stop destroying it. When in the woods, follow the rule "Take only pictures, leave only footprints." -- That is only a start though.

Photo by Chad Minter

Brad Kalota photographs an Eastern Coachwhip (Masticophis flagellum) in South Georgia.

Myths & Folktales

Snakes have been a source of myth, fantasy, and lore since the beginning of human civilization.

Long before the Bald Eagle graced our money and insignia, the National Symbol for the Thirteen Colonies was the Timber Rattlesnake. Our Forefathers marched under a flag which proudly displayed a Timber Rattlesnake cut into thirteen pieces, (from the idea that a snake cut could unite its parts again) and the banner "Don't Tread On Me."

Many cultures honor the snake and believe it to have magical or supernatural powers. The Hindus believed cobras were magical and still honor them with festivals. In some Asian temples, vipers crawl free and are considered a sign of good luck by their Buddhist caretakers. According to legend, the King Cobra saw The Buddha meditating under the Banyan Tree in a rainstorm and coiled under him to support his body. The cobra then spread its massive hood over him to protect him from the rain. Some tribes in Africa consider venomous snakes to be the holiest of creatures and killing one would be punishable by death. Even today in America, there exist a few Pentecostal churches who handle highly venomous snakes as a testament of faith.

Snakes are docile and non-confrontational by nature. Venom is a valuable resource to snakes in procuring their food. Given the chance to escape, a snake will most certainly choose flight over wasting its valuable venom on you.

Let's proceed with some myth-busting; All of the following statements are **true**;

- Rattlesnakes **do not** get their poison by sucking it out of hornet nests.
  Venom is a modified saliva produced in a gland above and behind the snake's eyes. It is carried to the fangs by a duct in their upper jaw.

- There **is not** a poisonous dust in a Rattlesnakes rattle.

  If there were dust in their rattles, it would muffle the sound made by the rattle. The only thing toxic about a rattlesnake is the venom.

- At least in the U.S., venomous snakes **do not** chase people.

  There are a couple of exotic species that have been known to advance on humans, two of which are nesting female King Cobras (Ophiophagus hannah) and Black Mambas (Dendroaspis polylepis) U.S. native venomous snakes simply will not do it.

- Cottonmouths **can** bite under water.

  Cottonmouths feed mainly on fish and frogs. They wouldn't be very good at catching fish and frogs if they couldn't bite under water.

- Baby venomous snakes **are** venomous at birth, and dangerous.

  While a baby venomous snake is not capable of delivering as high a dose of venom as a full grown adult, they are born with fully functional fangs, venom, and the ability in some species to deliver a deadly bite. Always treat any venomous snake with respect and keep a safe distance

Photo by Chad Minter

Snakes aren't the only venomous animals in the Southeastern U.S. This scorpion was found under a board on a farm in Georgia. They can deliver a powerful sting, along with a risk of anaphylactic reactions -- and should only be handled like this by trained arachnologists.

• A snake with a triangular head **is not** necessarily venomous.

Coral snakes (Micrurus sp.) do not have triangular heads, and several non-venomous snakes, including male brown water snakes (Nerodia taxispilota) do have triangular heads. In addition to this, many exotic species are venomous with slim heads, and many exotic species also are non-venomous with triangular heads.

• The fellow whose uncle was water skiing and fell into a nest of cottonmouths **is** just joshing you.

*That uncle has way too many nephews who can't produce a medical report or verifiable account to have ever existed. Cottonmouths **don't** nest.*

• Coral snakes **can** bite <u>without</u> having to chew or bite you between the fingers.

They are fully capable of producing a deadly bite anywhere on your body.

• Snakes **will** cross horse-hair ropes.

Most snake repellants work about as well as snake oils.

• Hanging a dead snake in a tree has **never** been proven to produce rain.

This is just an old wive's tale.

• Rat snakes **do not** become venomous if they eat a toad.

Toads themselves are poisonous -- in that they secrete a toxin through glands in their skin. It is not deadly, but apparently has a very bad taste. Dogs who have inadvertently picked up a toad may have a very adverse reaction to the toxins.

• You **cannot** tell a rattlesnake's age by the number of rattles.

Rattlesnakes add a new segment each time they shed their skin, this can be anywhere from one to four times a year. Rattles often break off.

• Snakes **don't** swallow their young to protect them.

Some species will eat other snakes including their own species if they are hungry but certainly not to protect them.

- Snakes **aren't** slimy.

   They are smooth and dry like tire rubber, and many people actually like the texture.

- There is **no** 'hoop snake' that will roll down a hill and stab you with its tail.

   Some snakes, such as Mud Snakes, have a modified scale at the tip of the tail that it can prod with, but it won't break the skin. There are no snakes with 'stingers' on their tails.

- Snakes **can** strike from any position.

   They don't have to be coiled. A snake can launch a much more effective strike from a coiled position, but don't count on the snake missing. Snakes have very fast and accurate strikes.

- Removing the fangs will **not** make a snake harmless.

   Snakes will quickly grow new ones, and many have spare fangs ready to drop into place at a moment's notice.

Photo by Chad Minter

Snake hunting in the mountains of the Carolinas. Timber Rattlesnakes and Copperheads are common in areas like this.

- Rattlesnakes **do** regularly shed their fangs.
  Keepers find them regularly while cleaning enclosures.

- Snakes **do not** steal milk from cows.
  Snakes drink only water.

- Snakes **do not** have poisonous breath.
  Again, the only thing toxic about a venomous snake is its venom.

- Snakes **cannot** 'charm' their prey.
  While an encounter with a snake will often have a bone-chilling effect on a person who is afraid of them, they have no hypnotic powers over people or prey.

- A snake that has been chopped in two **will not** grow into two new snakes, and the pieces **cannot** reattach themselves.
  The snake will simply die.

- Rattlesnakes **do not** always rattle before they strike.
  Many times a snake's first reaction in the wild is to freeze and stay perfectly still in the hopes that its camouflage will save it from any threat. Only after a snake is sure that you know it is there, and sometimes not even then, will it rattle as a warning. The safest thing to do if you are in the wild and hear a rattle is to stay perfectly still and find out exactly where that rattle is coming from. You don't want to jump backwards and land on another snake! Only when you know exactly where the rattler is, then should you turn and walk away carefully.

Snakebite

- About 8,000 Venomous Snakebites are reported each year in the U.S.
- Only 8-10 of these are fatal.
- 70% of venomous snakebites involve alcohol.
- 80% of venomous snakebites in the U.S. occur on the hand or forearm.
- 98% of venomous snakebites in the U.S. are attributed to Pit Vipers (Rattlesnakes, Cottonmouths, Copperheads)
- The chance of dying from a venomous snakebite in the U.S. is 1 in 10,000,000
- As many as 50% of rattlesnake bites are 'dry bites' where no venom is injected.
- More people are killed each year by lightning strikes than by venomous snakebites.
- More people are killed each year by bee stings than by venomous snakebites.
- More people are killed each year by dog attacks than by venomous snakebites.
- More people are killed each year by electrocution than by venomous snakebites.
- More people are killed each year in their own bathtubs than by venomous snakebites.

In every single story about a bite by a captive snake that I've heard, the story always starts the same "I was reaching in the cage and..."

Chris Harper

First Aid

The information included in this chapter is provided by named sources. The author makes no claim to proper procedures involving snakebite, nor has documented medical training pertaining to snakebite. In all instances of snakebite, the author suggests immediately securing proper medical treatment by qualified medical physicians. In no way is the author responsible for any results of snakebite, or snakebite treatment, as documented in this publication.

"The best snakebite kit is a set of car keys." A bite by a venomous snake is a *serious medical emergency.* Many people have severely injured themselves with unnecessary first aid procedures. Since most bites occur on the hand and forearm, if one attempts to 'cut and suck' they risk severing one of the many nerves or tendons that run just underneath the skin of the hand.

One medical professional told an account of a girl that had been bitten by a baby copperhead while cleaning a pool filter. Thinking that she had only minutes to live unless she performed the infamous 'cut and suck' procedure, she grabbed the nearest sharp object -- a rusty screwdriver -- and proceeded to gouge at her palm. She did far worse damage with the screwdriver than the venom of a baby copperhead would have done. She should have simply followed the advice of the CDC:

According to the Centers for Disease Control, if a bite by a venomous snake occurs:

• **Do remain calm - Remember that there is an excellent chance for survival, and in most cases there is plenty of time.**

• **Do suck and squeeze - as much venom as possible directly from the wound. Venom is protein and can be taken orally with no ill effects.**

• **Do remove jewelry - Swelling can progress rapidly, so rings, watches and bracelets can be a real problem.**

• **Do mark the time - The progress of symptoms (swelling) is the most obvious indicator of the amount of envenomation.**

• **Do keep the stricken limb below the heart.**

• **Do get to a hospital as quickly as possible - Anti-venom serum is the only sure cure for envenomation, and because some people are allergic to horse serum it should only be given in a fully equipped** medical facility.

• In case of a Coral bite, do pull the snake off immediately - Corals' fangs are relatively small, and they have to work at getting venom into the wound. Therefore, the faster the snake is removed the less venom is injected.

• Do attempt to identify the offending snake - Positive identification in the form of a dead snake is helpful, if convenient, but no time or safety should be wasted since the symptoms will give medical personnel an accurate diagnosis.

• Do get a tetanus shot.

Don't

• Don't cut the wound - This almost always causes more damage than it's worth.

• Don't use a tourniquet - This isolates the venom in a small area and causes the digestive enzymes in the venom to concentrate the damage.

• Don't use alcohol orally - it speeds the heart and blood flow and reduces the body's counter-acting ability.

• Don't use ice - Freezing the stricken limb has been found to be a major factor leading to amputation.

Venom

Snakes are not poisonous, they are venomous. A venom is injected. A poison is ingested or infused. Wasps, scorpions, lion-fish and rattlesnakes are venomous. Dart-frogs, certain mushrooms, and rotten cups of yogurt are poisonous.

Snake Venom is a modified saliva which is produced in a venom gland above and behind the eyes of the snake. It travels through ducts located in the upper jaw to a pair of hollow enlarged teeth called fangs. Venom is delivered in much the same way that a doctor gives an injection.

Venom is an extremely complex mixture of proteins and enzymes. Hemotoxic venom works by breaking down cells and tissue. Neurotoxic venom works by attacking the central nervous system. Snake venoms have different ratios of Hemotoxic and Neurotoxic components. The exact ratios vary by species, locality, health of the snake, and many other factors. A prime example of the complexity of venom is that venom may also contain neurotoxins, myotoxins, procoagulants, anticoagulants, hemorrhagins, nephrotoxins, cardiotoxins, necrotoxins, and many other compounds. *(www.toxinology.com)*

Venomous snakebites rarely consist of the two neat puncture wounds pictured in many manuals. Massive swelling, bleeding, blood blisters, and necrosis (a rotting-away of the flesh) quickly follow envenomations, especially in envenomations by pit vipers. Only one fang mark may be present. Numerous small punctures from the small teeth behind the fangs may be present.

Depending upon species, snakebite may also include symptoms such as headache, nausea, vomiting, abdominal pain, diarrhea, dizzyness, collapse, convulsions, pain, sweating, hyper-salivation, tearing, muscle fasciculation, high blood pressure, tingling sensations, filling of the lungs

Photo by Chad Minter

Rusty tin and fallen buildings can be a haven for snakes -- venomous and nonvenomous. When working around debris such as this, one should be very careful and observe all safety precautions.

with fluid, cardiac arrest, kidney failure, internal and external hemor-rhaging, paralysis, anaphylaxis, cyanosis, and/or death.

Antivenin is usually produced by giving an animal (in some cases, horses and sheep) controlled injections of snake venom. When the ani-mal has built up a sufficient immunity to the actions of the venom, blood is drawn from the animal. Antivenins are then extracted from the blood of the animal. Antivenin is a noun which describes the chemical itself. Antivenom is an adjective describing the chemical's effects upon venom.

Many people have allergic reactions to venom. Many people also have allergic reactions to the antivenin. Exposure to either one increases the chances of developing a sensitivity. If you have been bitten before, received antivenin before, or are exposed to venomous snakes on a reg-ular basis, this increases your chances of having an allergic reaction and it would be wise to talk to your physician about what medications to carry in case of exposure to the same chemicals again.

Anaphylaxis is an extremely severe allergic reaction. One of the symptoms of anaphylaxis is swelling of the pharynx. This can result in

the inability of the person to breathe. Anaphylaxis is serious and can result in death within a matter of minutes.

Many things can affect the severity of a venomous snakebite. The age, weight, and health of the victim are major factors. The loca-tion on the body where the bite occurs, the depth of the bite, and the amount of venom injected are also important. Snakes can control the amount of venom they inject. In many cases they do not inject any venom at all. Many folk reme-dies for snakebite came about because someone received a dry

Photo by Chad Minter

When lifting doors, plywood, or other debris use a tool and don't stick your fingers underneath. Lift the door up toward you, so the door is between your legs and the snake under it.

bite. The species, age, and health of the snake is also a determining factor in the severity of a snakebite. The sensitivity level of the person bitten is important, as is whether they have been bitten before, been exposed to antivenin before, or even been exposed to snakes themselves. People allergic to horses and horse proteins, and people allergic to sheep and sheep proteins, are much more likely to have an allergic reaction following a bite or treatment. A person's own psychological and physical reaction to a bite situation can greatly affect the severity of the bite. A person who is calm and inactive after a bite will generally fare much better than a person who is upset or very active after a bite.

Avoiding a Bite

There are several things a homeowner can do to minimize the appeal of their yard to venomous snakes.

First and foremost, DON'T KILL NONVENOMOUS SNAKES. Any given area can only support a fixed number of snakes. For every non-venomous snake in your yard, that is one venomous snake that you do not have. The non-venomous snakes use the food supply which could easily support a population of rattlesnakes.

Many non-venomous snakes also kill venomous snakes. While kingsnakes regularly kill and eat rattlesnakes, such harmless snakes as Rat Snakes and Indigo Snakes have also been recorded to prey upon smaller venomous snakes.

Second, try to control rodents. If there is no food source in an area, a snake will quickly leave for more suitable hunting grounds. Bird feeders are notorious for attracting snakes. Birds, squirrels, and rodents feed on the spilled seeds. Dander and urine from the small birds and mammals quickly attracts snakes.

Third, pick up debris. Pieces of plywood, lumber, siding, tin, old refrig-

*Most snakebites occur when someone
tries to catch or kill a snake.*

The safest thing you can do if you see a snake is to leave it alone.

erators, and just about anything we can think to leave laying around can be utilized by a snake as cover.

Fourth, cut the grass. Snakes don't like to be in the open. They like a sense of security and the ability to hide from predators. A yard overgrown with ivy and knee-high grass can be a perfect sanctuary for a snake.

If you see a snake...

If you see a snake, the best thing to do is leave it alone. <u>Most bites occur when someone tries to catch or kill a snake.</u> In the United States, more than 80% of bites occur on the hand and forearm, 70% involve a measurable blood alcohol content, and the most common victim is a young male. This makes it painfully obvious that the biggest mistake someone can make in dealing with a venomous snake is to try to handle it in an improper manner. If you have not been professionally trained in handling venomous snakes, don't do it!

Never try to pick up a dead snake. A snake's reflexes still function after death and the animal is fully capable of delivering a deadly bite. My only envenomation was by a dead Canebrake Rattlesnake. Treat dead snakes the same way you would treat live snakes. Wounded animals are much more likely to bite out of fear than healthy animals.

Watch where you step and where you put your hands. Snakes will bite for two reasons, fear and food. If a snake is under a piece of plywood, and it senses your fingers suddenly appear, it might mistake your finger for a mouse. If you step onto a snake, the snake might misidentify your innocent mistake for an attack and defend itself. Venomous snakes are well equipped for self-defense.

Step onto logs rather than over them. Snakes will sit coiled on or beside logs waiting for prey to pass by, in what is known as "the Reinert posture." When your leg appears out of nowhere it could be perceived as prey or even an attack.

Wear leg protection and baggy pants. A loose fitting pants leg can cause a snake to prematurely close its mouth during a strike.

Stay a safe distance away from the snake. Even though a snake usually only strikes about 3/4 of their body length, they can strike farther under some circumstances. There is also a possibility that you may trip and fall within strike range.

There are some simple and safe ways to remove a snake from your yard. The easiest and safest way is to call someone who is trained in their removal. If you need to keep the snake in one place till help arrives, a large rubbermaid trash can can be placed upside-down over the snake and held in place with a weight or cinder block.

Another safe way to get snakes to leave is to stand at a distance of at least ten feet and spray the snake with a garden hose. Snakes don't like to be sprayed, and will leave immediately.

Classification & Identification

Snakes are members of the kingdom Animalia, phylum Chordata, class Reptilia, order Squamata, and sub-order Serpentes. There are approximately 3,000 species of snakes worldwide. Approximately 300 species of venomous snakes exist worldwide. Six venomous species occur in the Southeastern United States; These six are the Eastern Diamondback Rattlesnake (*Crotalus adamanteus*), The Timber/ Canebrake Rattlesnake (*Crotalus horridus*), The Pigmy Rattlesnake (*Sistrurus miliarius*), The Cottonmouth (*Agkistrodon piscivorus*), the Copperhead (*Agkistrodon contortrix*), and the Eastern Coral Snake (*Micrurus fulvius.*)

Taxonomic Issues

Why Latin Names?

Latin names are necessary in the world of herpetology. They eliminate confusion, and in some cases can save human lives. Common names are good, but they vary from region to region and country to country. For each species there is but one latin name.

A man of the past century would call a harmless hognose snake a "Puff Adder."

A man of modern times would call a dangerous viper from Africa a "Puff Adder."

A doctor treating a snakebite needs to hear "Heterodon platyrhinos," referring to the harmless hognose snake, or "Bitis arietans," referring to the dangerous viper, to know which course of treatment to follow and whether or not to prescribe antivenin.

In today's information age we can instantly communicate with other snake enthusiasts around the world. Latin names remain constant no matter what language you speak, where you live, or who you are. They are both beneficial and necessary.

The task may seem daunting, but, if you are truly interested in herpetology, use them. Learn them one at a time. No matter with whom you talk, both parties will always be able to understand exactly which species you are discussing. You will become more and more comfortable using latin names as your knowledge grows.

Please forgive a moment of technical jargon, but for the herpetologists who would pounce upon someone for using the term "Canebrake Rattlesnake" an explanation is necessary. In the 1930's the southern variation of the Timber Rattlesnake was given subspecies status, and it was called *Crotalus horridus atricaudatus*. In the 1970's this subspecies was deemed invalid and the 'Canebrake Rattlesnake' was then just *Crotalus horridus* again.

Photo by Derek Egolf

A gravid female Timber Rattlesnake in the Pennsylvania Mountains

There is much debate about the validity of the subspecies *Crotalus horridus atricaudatus*. Pisani did a study and concluded that no such subspecies exists. Brown and Ernst repeated the same study and found that there was significant enough differences between *C. horridus horridus* and *C. horridus atricaudatus* to warrant subspeciation in North/South populations. Clark recently completed a study of mitochondrial DNA and concluded there are two distinct lineages, divided along the East/West portions of the range. (*Ernst, Carl, Venomous Reptiles of North America, 1992, Smithsonian Institution Press; Clark, Ginger, 2003, personal communication with the author*)

This is quite confusing, and debate is both common and heated among professional herpetologists. Unless shown a convincing reason for lumping the two together as one subspecies, this author is going to take the common sense approach and say "Regardless of what name you give them; they look different, act different, live in different habitats, have different scalation, and different venom compositions then they are obviously different."

Photo by Chad Minter

A Canebrake Rattlesnake in the South Georgia swamps.

Whether one considers *C. horridus atricaudatus* to be a valid subspecies in the world of taxonomy, or just a regional variation, there is little doubt that the two color variations are different and recognizable. For this writing, a distinction between the two is needed. The common names of Timber Rattlesnake and Canebrake Rattlesnake will suffice. When speaking of both, the term Timber/Canebrake will be used.

Timber Rattlesnakes are darker in color, reach an adult length of four feet, prefer rocky outcrops in high altitudes, and have a less potent venom than their southern counterparts.

Canebrake Rattlesnakes are lighter in color, regularly reach lengths of 5 to 6 feet, prefer lowland swampy areas, and have a much more potent venom than their northern counterparts.

Species Accounts
Eastern Diamondback Rattlesnake
Crotalus adamanteus

The latin *Crotalus* translates as "rattle tail," and *adamanteus* translates as "diamondlike pattern."

Eastern Diamondback Rattlesnakes are found from the Carolinas in the East, throughout Florida in the South, and West to Louisiana. While North Carolina protects the diamondback as a native species, their physical presence in the state is almost non-existant.

Eastern Diamondback Rattlesnakes prefer sandy scrub along the coastal plains. They often take shelter in the burrows of the Gopher Tortoise during the heat of the day or at night. Diamondbacks move more often in the mornings before 10:00 a.m.

Eastern Diamonbacks are proficient swimmers. They have been seen miles offshore, moving between barrier islands.

Eastern Diamondbacks are very temperature sensitive and prefer to move when the temperatures are 68-78 degrees. If the temperature reaches the mid-80's, most diamondbacks are going to seek out deep cover or underground burrows.

The Eastern Diamondback Rattlesnake is a large, heavy bodied pit

Photo by Chad Minter

A coiled snake can strike up, back, and in any direction... even around corners. Notice the "S" curve in the neck, like a coiled spring ready to strike. A Rattlesnakes head has been clocked at over 150 miles per hour in mid-strike.

viper which may grow to over six feet in length and weigh in excess of 15 pounds. Record lengths of eight foot specimens exist, but are rare. Eastern Diamondback Rattlesnakes over six feet in length are seldom encountered.

Eastern Diamondback Rattlesnakes feed on small mammals and birds. Throughout most of their range their diet consists largely of Quail and Cottontail Rabbits. The young feed mainly on mice and small rats.

Eastern Diamondback Rattlesnakes breed in the spring and the fall. Females give live birth to up to 20 babies, usually in September or October. The young may spend up to the first three years of their life underground in stump holes, root systems, and tortoise burrows. They are around 12 inches long when born. Under normal circumstances, the young grow approximately 12

Photo by Chad Minter

An Eastern Diamondback Rattlesnake found on an abandoned farm coiled under a rusty gas tank.

inches in length per year for the first three years of their life. A shed skin can be used to determine the sex of an Eastern Diamondback. Males have 26+ subcaudal scutes posterior to the cloacal opening. Females have 25 or less subcaudal scutes posterior to the cloacal opening. This method does not work for all species of rattlesnakes, but it is very reliable for Eastern Diamondbacks.

Photo by Cyndi Betz

A large Eastern Diamondback Rattlesnake being safely removed from a walking trail by Karl H. Betz.

Eastern Diamondback Rattlesnakes are often killed for sport, skins, parts, and out of fear and hatred. Gall bladders are used in asian medicine as a virility aid.

Photo by Chad Minter

An Eastern Diamondback Rattlesnake found on a South Georgia farm. Notice the flicking tongue. Snakes pick up particles with their tongue from the air and use the Jacobson's Organ in the roof of their mouth to 'smell.'

Rattlesnakes are commercially collected for rattlesnake roundups, kept for months without food or water in cramped and unsuitable conditions, milked on public display, then killed and skinned. The venom collected at these tragic events is not useful for the production of antivenin.

In addition to being the largest venomous snake in the U.S., and having the longest fangs of any snake in the U.S., Eastern Diamondback Rattlesnakes produce the largest volume of venom. A fully grown Eastern Diamondback can produce 6 to 9 times the amount of venom necessary to kill a grown man.

Symptoms of a Diamondback envenomation include sweating, pain, chills, nausea, vomiting, dizziness, numbness, hypersalivation, thirst, blurred vision, unconsciousness, partial paralysis, kidney failure, and death.

Death can occur in a few hours, or in the case of allergic reactions (anaphylaxis), within a few minutes. People who have previously been bitten, who work with snakes on a regular basis, or who have received antivenin before are at a much higher risk of having an allergic reaction

Photo by Derek Egolf

A Sad Day -- After looking for diamondbacks all day long, we came across this snake, barely alive, which had been beaten with the log shown. It died a few minutes after we found it.

to a bite.

Bites by Eastern Diamondbacks often require extensive medical treatment including surgeries, dozens of vials of antivenin (up to 100 vials in some cases,) and may require weeks or months of hospitalization.

One individual was bitten by a four foot Eastern Diamondback in a cage cleaning accident. The bite required a fasciotomy, which is a surgery to relieve pressure when the hand was swollen to the point that the skin was about to burst. Controlled cuts were made to prevent random tearing of tissue. The bite required 30 vials of antivenin, the man went into kidney failure and stopped breathing twice. This bite was unique in that it showed major neurotoxic symptoms with very little tissue destruction.

It has been speculated in recently published papers that rattlesnake venom is evolving, and is becoming more neurotoxic.

Eastern Diamondback venom is a mixture of hemotoxins and neurotoxins. The individuals from the northern parts of their range show a much higher level of neurotoxins but these levels can vary according to many factors including age, health of the snake, locality, and can even vary between members of the same litter. Some people theorize that populations with higher neurotoxins have evolved because of a diet consisting mainly of birds. High neurotoxins would prevent a bitten bird from flying away before the meal could be consumed.

Species Accounts
Timber/Canebrake Rattlesnake
Crotalus horridus ssp.

Common names for Timber Rattlesnakes include timber, canebrake, smut-tail, and seminole rattler. The latin Crotalus translates as "rattle-tail," and horridus translates as "horrible." Crotalus horridus atricaudatus translates as "horrible rattle-tail black-tail."

Timber Rattlesnakes are found throughout most of the Eastern United States and in every state in the Southeastern U.S. The populations are clustered, and one area may be completely devoid of their presence, while an adjoining area may have thriving populations.

Timber Rattlesnakes prefer to frequent rocky outcrops at high elevations. Their lowland brethren, the Canebrake Rattlesnake prefers moist low lying habitat such as the areas surrounding swamps. Abandoned farmland often plays host to numerous Canebrake Rattlesnakes. Tin and fallen shacks provide shelter and a steady supply of rodents.

The Timber Rattlesnake population is severely depleted in much of its former range. This species is protected in many states. The Timber Rattlesnake was proposed as a candidate for the Convention on International Trade in Endangered Species a few years ago. It did not pass because of the high numbers of Canebrake Rattlesnakes in the south. Populations of the Timber Rattlesnake in other areas remain threatened.

Timber Rattlesnakes are variable in pattern and coloration. Their coloration ranges from a dark black to an extremely vivid yellow. The pat-

Photo by Chad Minter
A captive raised Canebrake Rattlesnake from a West Georgia locality. This snake was raised from a baby by the author. Despite being raised in captivity, it has never adjusted to a human presence and is more than willing to bite and envenomate if ever given the chance.

tern is similar to the Canebrake Rattlesnake and includes the same crossing chevrons. In most Timber Rattlesnakes the vertebral stripe is lacking, barely visible, or only present during the youth of the snake. An average adult length of four feet is common.

Canebrake Rattlesnakes are lighter in color than the Timber Rattlesnakes. Their vertebral stripe is well defined. Adults regularly reach a length of five to six feet.

Timber/Canebrake Rattlesnakes feed almost exclusively on small mammals and birds.

Breeding occurs in the fall. Sperm is stored over the winter. Ovulation occurs in the spring. 8-12 live young are born the next fall. This cycle is repeated, producing a litter of babies every other year for only two to three years of the female's life. This is a small number of offspring compared to many snakes, and even one of these will be lucky to make it to adulthood in the wild.

Canebrakes tend to *appear* very calm and placid. Many times they have been caught, bagged, caged, fed, and never rattled once during the ordeal. This can be the downfall of someone who is not well versed in their behavior. While appearing calm and placid, if given the chance to bite they will explode into a full strike. Phil, a longtime friend and avid herpetologist, named his Canebrake Rattlesnake 'PipeBomb' because of its propensity to do just that. Timber/Canebrake Rattlesnakes are very dangerous to handle. They are unpredictable and quite capable of delivering a very deadly dose of venom.

Animals from the southernmost part of their range have the highest levels of neurotoxins. According to one expert, a population in South Georgia shows levels as high as 37% neurotoxins. This rivals the Mojave Rattlesnake (*Crotalus scutulatus*.) The Mojave is a western rattlesnake often considered to deliver the most dangerous bite of the North American rattlesnakes.

While Canebrake bites are more serious than Timber bites due to the potent venom and high levels of neurotoxins, both are serious and life threatening bites. More than three cases of bites by this species within the last few years resulted in death in less than an hour. Most bites allow for 2 to 3 hours to for medical treatment, but don't count on it.

Species Accounts
Pigmy Rattlesnake
Sistrurus miliarius

Pigmy Rattlesnakes (*Sistrurus miliarius*) are known colloquially as ground rattlers and buzz worms. The latin Sistrurus translates as "rattle," and miliarius translates as "millet-like pattern."

Pigmy Rattlesnakes range throughout the Southeastern Coastal Plain from the Carolinas, through Florida and Georgia, and west to Texas, Oklahoma, and Arkansas. Pigmy Rattlesnakes are found along the southeast coastal plain in sandy soil, often in palmetto scrub. They prefer semi-moist areas where frogs are plentiful. Pigmy Rattlesnakes are generally the most abundant venomous snake in the areas where they occur.

Pigmy Rattlesnakes are small snakes which rarely exceed two feet in length and fifteen inches is a normal adult size. Specimens of 30 inches in length are reported but not common. (See the photo of Mardi Snipes displaying an

Photo by Chad Minter
A Dusky Pigmy Rattlesnake coiled among oak leaves outside the Okefenokee Swamp in South Georgia. Pigmy Rattlesnakes are abundant in areas that they occur. Roughly half of all snakebites in Florida are attributed to Pigmy Rattlesnakes.

abnormally large Dusky Pigmy Rattlesnake.) Pigmy Rattlesnakes are between three and four inches at birth, and can coil comfortably on the surface of an American Quarter with room left over.

Pigmy rattlesnakes are variable in ground color, and can have one, two, or three rows of spots depending on subspecies. The rattles are fragile and tend to break off, so they are not always present. Their rattles are more slender than the rattles of the other two species of rattlesnake native to the Southeast. The head is covered with nine enlarged plates, whereas Eastern Diamondbacks and Timber/Canebrake Rattlesnakes have heads which are covered with smaller scales.

Young Pigmy Rattlesnakes are born with a yellow or white tail, which they use as a caudal lure to attract prey. This darkens as the snake matures.

There are three subspecies of Pigmy Rattlesnake; The Carolina Pigmy Rattlesnake (*Sistrurus miliarius miliarius,*) the Dusky Pigmy Rattlesnake (*Sistrurus miliarius barbouri*) and the Western Pigmy Rattlesnake (*Sistrurus miliarius streckeri.*) All three are similar in appearance. The Dusky Pigmy Rattlesnake is distinguished by three rows of spots on each side, the Carolina Pigmy Rattlesnake has two rows of spots on each side, and the Western Pigmy Rattlesnake has

Photo by Matt King

A Carolina Pigmy Rattlesnake from Northeast Georgia. Caging for venomous snakes needs to be secure, escape proof, and lockable. Caring for captive venomous reptiles is rewarding, but should only be attempted after an apprenticeship under a skilled handler.

only one row of spots on each side.

Young Pigmy Rattlers feed mainly on small frogs and lizards, but their diet may also include insects, centipedes, and other snakes. When mature, their diet often switches to small mice or young rats.

One particularly interesting behavior is that Pigmy Rattlesnakes will feed readily upon cricket frogs, *Acris gryllus*, but when a Pigmy Rattlesnake bites a spring peeper, *Pseudacris crucifer*, they generally let go of it fast and have a reaction as though the frog were quite distasteful.

Photo by Chad Minter
"That's Some Pig!" This Pigmy Rattlesnake is owned by Mardi Snipes, of Coastal Reptiles. It is over 30 inches and may be a world record.

Pigmy Rattlesnakes breed in the spring and the fall. Babies are born in late summer. Numbers of offspring are dependent upon the size and weight of the mother, but often average from 4 to 12. Baby Pigmy Rattlesnakes are born alive, and often do not eat for the first three or four weeks after birth.

Pigmy Rattlesnake bites are extremely painful. Their venom is highly effective on mammals, and kill-times for mice are measured in seconds rather than minutes. Their venom seems to be hemorrhagic in nature and bites result in swelling, pain, respiratory distress and nausea; renal failure has been reported in at least one bite. Death is quite possible in humans. While the author could find no verifiable human deaths from Pigmy Rattlesnake bites, the high toxicity coupled with the possiblity of evolving venoms make this a very dangerous bite. As with any venom, the possibility of allergic reactions is always present. A bite would require immediate medical attention by a licensed and experienced physician.

Pigmy Rattlesnakes are one of the most abundant venomous snakes in some areas of the Southeast. Around half of the snakebites reported in Florida are attributed to pigmy rattlesnakes. Several bites have occurred in the garden centers at large retail stores due to Pigmy Rattlesnakes taking refuge in potted plants before they are shipped there from the nurseries.

Pigmy Rattlesnakes frequent low shrubs in search of lizards, and can be found several feet off the ground. They are often found coiled on top of fallen logs and tree stumps.

Pigmy Rattlesnakes are most often encountered in September, when males begin to crawl in search of mates.

Species Accounts
Cottonmouth
Agkistrodon contortrix

Agkistrodon piscivorous is known colloquially as the Cottonmouth, Water Moccasin, and Trap-jaw. The latin *Agkistrodon* translates as "hooked tooth," and *piscivorus* translates as "fish eater."

Cottonmouths are found throughout the Southeastern Coastal Plains. Their presence seems to be affected most by suitable habitat, altitude, and availability of food. The Western subspecies is much less affected by altitude and can be found much farther north than its Eastern and Florida counterparts.

Cottonmouths generally prefer habitat near water in lowland swamp areas, and occasionally bask on branches over the water. They are much less temperature sensitive than other snakes. They can be found out basking in the Winter in Georgia and Florida, even in temperatures as

Photo by Chad Minter
This Cottonmouth from the Okefenokee Swamp in South Georgia was a Florida Cottonmouth (Agkistrodon piscivorus conanti.) There are three subspecies of Cottonmouth, Eastern, Western, and Florida.

low as 50 degrees. Usually, though not all the time, Cottonmouths swim with their entire body floating on top of the surface of the water. Water snakes usually swim with their bodies submerged. If you see a snake swimming with its body above the surface of the water, and its head is held high, it is most likely a Cottonmouth.

Cottonmouths tend to hold their heads in a vertical position, as if they were star gazing, especially if a potential threat is in the vicinity.

Cottonmouths are usually not commercially collected. Their venom is valuable for use in the production of antivenin, and at least one common anti-coagulant heart medication is produced from their venom. Their numbers are more abundant than most species, due to their choice of habitat; swamps and rivers are not ideal locations for real estate development.

Cottonmouths are heavy bodied pit vipers that can reach lengths of up to six feet in length. Adult lengths of Cottonmouths are usually in the three foot range, but four foot specimens are fairly common. Five and six foot specimens are very rare. One roadkill cottonmouth found in South Georgia measured 5' 7".

Cottonmouths are often confused with Northern, Midland, Brown,

Photo by Chad Minter
This cottonmouth is displaying a typical defensive behavior of flattening its body, shaking its tail rapidly, and gaping its jaws to display the white lining of its mouth.

Banded, and Green Watersnakes. Large male Brown Watersnakes (*Nerodia taxispilota*) are so similar in build and shape to Cottonmouths that several herpetologists have caught them before realizing that they were not Cottonmouths until they were captured.

Watersnakes have a propensity to imitate cottonmouths. They will puff their bodies up, flatten their heads, and do a quite impressive impersonation of a venomous snake.

Cottonmouths feed mainly on fish and frogs, however they will readily take small mammals, birds, and other snakes, including their own species. Cottonmouths will often devour already

Photo by James Dean
This Cottonmouth found dead on a road in South Georgia measured 5 feet 6 inches.

killed prey. Tanith Tyrr gave an account of a Cottonmouth trying to pry a sunbaked and flattened road-kill frog from the asphalt on a Florida highway.

Cottonmouths produce 8-12 live young, usually born in the fall.

Like the copperhead and pigmy rattlesnake, baby cottonmouths have a bright yellow tail-tip which they use as a caudal lure to attract frogs and fish.

At least one case of parthenogenesis (reproduction without mating) has been recorded. A lone female kept at a reptile zoo in Georgia gave birth to two babies after having been in captivity for more than 5 years without any access to male cottonmouths. While it is plausible that this was sperm retention, it was more likely parthenogenesis. Parthenogenesis has been confirmed in at least one

Photo by Chad Minter
Proper tools and training are a must when handling venomous snakes. Here, Brad Kalota handles a Cottonmouth with common sense and safety in mind

other species of pit viper, and many species of lizards. The babies remained unusually small though they ate well. Their skulls also seemed to be slightly deformed.

Cottonmouth venom is highly hemotoxic. Massive tissue destruction and secondary infections, coupled with the possibility of allergic reactions make this a very dangerous bite. A high percentage of their bites produce massive necrosis, and often end in amputation. Human deaths from their bite are rare, but are serious medical emergencies and would require immediate medical attention from a licensed and experienced physician.

Cottonmouths are calm, placid, and reluctant to bite. Their reputation as the denizen of southern swamps is wholly inaccurate and undeserved. At the end of the nineteenth and the beginning of the twentieth century, logging was allowed in the Okeefneokee Swamp. During this time, not a single logger was bitten by a cottonmouth.

I would certainly like to, but probably never will, meet the big aggressive cottonmouth which seems to chase so many frightened people from the swamps.

According to one fellow a Cottonmouth chased him all the way

Photo by Chad Minter

Alligators love snakes -- for lunch! This 7 foot American Alligator was lounging along the outskirts of the Okefenokee Swamp in South Georgia. They have been seen eating cottonmouths.

home, came up the steps and was only stopped when the man slammed the kitchen door on the snake, cutting the snake in half. I wish I could have been there to see it, because I have yet to meet a snake that would do it.

One cottonmouth behavior that is often confused with aggression is their propensity to climb into boats. From a Cottonmouth's point of view, as he is swimming along, a canoe or small boat looks amazingly like a nice fat log on which to rest.

Photo by Chad Minter

This Watersnake is flattening its body and head to appear menacing in hopes that the author would think it was a cottonmouth and leave it alone.

Imagine his surprise when he is met by a whack on the head from a boat paddle when he climbs out of the water!

Captive specimens are usually well adjusted, and seem to know when they are getting a 'free ride.' They quickly learn who their keepers are and that they are in no danger. While the occasional spastic specimen will not lose its propensity to bite, most are genuinely calm.

This has been confirmed by research done by Dr. Whit Gibbons at U.G.A. Dr. Gibbons used an artificial human arm to determine how venomous snakes reacted in the wild to encounters with humans. He found that of the six native venomous species, cottonmouths were the least likely to bite when touched.

Again, even though they are not aggressive animals, their bite is very dangerous. Do not take chances by trying to capture or kill them.

Species Accounts
Copperhead
Agkistrodon contortrix

Agkistrodon contortrix is known colloquially as the Copperhead, Highland Moccasin, and Chunkhead. The latin *Agkistrodon* translates as "hooked tooth," and *contortrix* translates as "twisted pattern."

Copperheads are found in virtually the entire Southeastern U.S. Their range barely touches into the Florida Panhandle but are prevalent over the rest of the Southeastern states.

Copperheads are very adaptable to varying habitats. They can be found on mountains in rocky outcrops where they share dens with Timber Rattlesnakes as well as in lowland swamp areas in the Southeast where they share haunts with Canebrake Rattlesnakes and Cottonmouths.

In some areas, Copperheads remain plentiful. However, in other areas their numbers have dropped dramatically. At least one state protects this species.

Copperheads are reddish-brown pit vipers that rarely exceed three

Photo by Zack Egolf
The loreal pit, an organ used to sense heat, is very obvious on this Northern Copperhead.

feet in length. An average adult size is 24 inches. One or two specimens per year are found that reach 40-48 inches. The best rule of thumb for identifying Southern Copperheads is that their pattern, when viewed from the side, resembles a row of Hershey's Kiss™ candies. Like the Cottonmouth, baby Copperheads have a bright sulfur yellow tail which they use as a caudal lure to attract prey.

When encountered in the field, Copperheads do not hesitate to bite. Many times they will blindly strike in random directions. They also have a habit of making mad dashes away in any direction without forethought. Catching copperheads is definitely an easy way to find yourself snake-bitten.

Copperheads feed mainly on birds and small mammals. Other prey has been reported by several researchers who regularly found cicadas in the stomachs of copperheads.

Photo by Chad Minter

A captive Southern Copperhead. Notice the bulbous swelling behind the eye at the back of the head. This is the venom gland. Also visible is the loreal pit between the eye and nostril. This is used as a heat sensing device to triangulate the position of prey.

Breeding occurs in the spring and fall. 8 to 30 live offspring are born in the fall. The number of offspring tends to be proportional to the body weight, age, and health of the female.

Copperheads are rarely commercially collected, but are often killed out of ignorance. Copperheads are valuable because several human medications are derived from their venom. One compound in particular, *contortrostatin*, has been shown to slow or stop the growth of cancer tumors in laboratory mice, and is currently being approved for human use.

Photo by Chad Minter

Harmless Corn Snakes are often confused with copperheads, and are needlessly killed.

Copperhead venom has been described as 'mild' by some herpetologists. They are underestimating this species. There have been at least two confirmed deaths from Copperhead bites. Most bites involve severe pain, swelling, nausea, vomiting, and limited local necrosis. Death is rare but not impossible. Copperhead bites resulting in amputations of fingers are not uncommon.

Photo by Chad Minter

A Southern Copperhead found in South Georgia

In describing the pain of a Copperhead bite, one medical professional told the story of a lady who was bitten in the leg by a moderately sized Copperhead. She said the pain of the bite was far worse than the pain of child birth.

Species Accounts
Eastern Coral Snake
Micrurus fulvius

Micrurus fulvius, the Eastern Coral Snake, is known colloquially as the Coral Snake or Harlequin Snake. The latin *Micrurus* translates as "small tail," and *fulvius* translates as "reddish-orange [bands]."

Coral Snakes are found along the sandy coastal plain from North Carolina, throughout Florida, Southern Georgia, Alabama, Mississippi, Louisiana and into Texas.

Coral Snakes spend a great deal of time underground, and emerge to feed at irregular intervals. They have been seen active at night and during the day, but most often after or during warm spring rains. They prefer sandy soil that is easy to burrow in. Rocky soil or soil high in clay content are usually devoid of Coral Snakes. While they are sometimes called nocturnal, they crawl in varied weather and at any time of day. Their behavior seems to neither have rhyme nor reason.

Coral Snakes have a number of defensive mechanisms to comple-

Photo by Chad Minter

The Eastern Coral Snake is the only member of the family elapidae that occurs in the Southeast United States. This family includes cobras, mambas, and kraits. Identification is easy -- a colorful red, yellow and black snake with a <u>black nose</u>.

ment their fangs and deadly venom. Coral Snakes will begin to move in one direction, then their heads will turn in the opposite direction so that they are crawling along the side of their own body. This movement coupled with their banded color pattern confuses the eye as to which direc-

tion the snake is actually moving. A predator aiming for where it thinks the snake is going to be is usually surprised to find that the snake is actually a couple of feet away.

Coral Snakes also have a habit of burying their head amongst leaves or their own body, curling their tail up, and waving it in the air. A predator grabbing this false head would most certainly find the other end of the Coral Snake latched onto its body injecting tiny amounts of very potent neurotoxins.

Photo by Jake Kable
The author handles an Eastern Coral Snake during an impromptu photo-shoot in South Georgia. Don't try this at home, kids!

One rare, but observed, reaction in the Coral Snake is to lift its head several inches off the ground in a manner similar to its cousin, the cobra. While it does not spread a hood, this seems to be a similar warning gesture, and is a typical elapid response to stress.

Coral Snakes can be as different as night and day. Some are calm and altogether perfect snakes. Others are nervous and drop food at the slightest movement.

There is very little information about population densities of Coral Snakes. Their secretive habits make them difficult to study. While they are rarely seen, they seem to be abundant in certain areas. Some commercial collectors have reported being able to pull 20 or more Coral Snakes from the highways in one area of Florida in one night. They do not do well in captivity. Though they often eat well, they rarely live over six months when confined. One individual owned by Delton Hilliard lived for over 13 years in captivity, but this is definitely an exception to the rule when it comes to these mysterious snakes.

Coral Snakes are flighty, nervous snakes. They do not 'strike' as a general rule. They tend to bite in a sideways motion. Coral Snake bites tend to occur when somone picks up the snake and plays with it.

Coral Snakes are thin, brightly colored snakes with red, yellow, and black bands. Usually the tail is missing the red bands and is only black and yellow. The nose is black. Coral Snakes are very similar in appearance to the nonvenomous Scarlet Snake and Scarlet Kingsnake. The Coral Snakes red and yellow bands touch each other and the nose is black, while the Scarlet and Scarlet Kingsnakes red and yellow bands do not touch each other and their nose is red. The rhyme **Red touch yellow, kill a fellow; Red touch black, friend to Jack** is often used as a mnemonic device, but it is much easier just to look for the black nose of the venomous Coral Snake.

A Coral Snake's diet consists mainly of other snakes, though sometimes they feed on small lizards. Captive Coral Snakes almost never feed upon mammals. It is thought by some that captive Coral Snakes don't thrive well because they may be missing some nutrient or bacteria that they would be exposed to in the wild.

Coral Snakes are the only egg-laying venomous snake in the U.S. Very little is known of their breeding habits in the wild due to their secretive and reclusive nature. They generally deposit four to five elongated eggs in rotten

Photo by Derek Egolf

This Scarlet Kingsnake looks very similar to an Eastern Coral Snake. The nose on the kingsnake is red, while the nose on Coral Snakes is black.

logs, sawdust piles, and possibly underground.

Coral Snakes are rarely commercially collected except for use by venom labs. Many harmless kingsnakes have met their death after being mistaken for the Coral Snake.

Coral snakes are the only North American members of the family elapidae which includes cobras and kraits. Like their cousins, the cobras, they have a pair of fixed front fangs. Their venom is highly neurotoxic and much more powerful than any of the pit vipers. The amount of venom usually delivered in one bite is small, but roughly the same amount as the lethal dose for one adult human.

No deaths have been attributed to Coral Snakes since the introduction of antivenin. Prior to antivenin, the death rate was approximately 10 percent. As of this writing only one company in North America is currently producing Coral Snake antivenin. This is Wyeth laboratories.

Symptoms of bites by Coral Snakes include, but are not limited to, pain, altered mental status, weakness, muscular fasciculations, respiratory difficulty, soft tissue swelling, difficulty swallowing, hypersalivation, and pharyngeal spasms. Severe bites may require intubation on a respirator.

Treatment usually consists of antivenin along with other medications for hypotension and the treatment of anaphylaxis, should it occur. It is important to understand that treatment must be administered by a licensed and experienced physician. Usually 3-10 vials of Coral Snake antivenin are used to treat a case of envenomation, but this may vary.

Coral Snake bites are often underestimated as to their severity. Coral Snake venom is unique in that symptoms sometimes do not appear until 4-12 hours after the bite. In some cases, bite victims went to the hospital and were released because they were asymptomatic. Only after being sent home and being told that they were mistaken as to the identity of the snake that bit them, did they begin to show symptoms of full blown envenomation.

A bite from a Coral Snake is a serious medical emergency and even a dry bite requires at least 24 hours of hospitalization, if for no reason other than observation.

Conclusion

In summary, it is my hope that the following goals have been met in writing this publication:

To point out the need for conservation.
Snakes are an integral part of the ecosystem. To preserve the ecosystem, we must preserve snakes. To preserve snakes we must preserve the ecosystem. When habitat is destroyed, snakes are displaced. When snakes are killed, the ecosystem is adversely affected. They go hand-in-hand. Without one, the other is not the same. When any predator is removed from an ecosystem, its prey (in this case rodents of all sizes) can multiply until its numbers reach dangerous proportions. Balance is a fragile thing. We must be mindful of conservation, and the best way to conserve something is to leave it alone.

To give the reader at least a peek into the fascinating world of snakes.
Snakes have been feared, worshipped, loathed, and loved throughout our history. Snakes are mysterious and fascinating creatures. Many of us are not lucky enough to live in an area where we can observe them in the wild. Hopefully, this book will be a keyhole through which we can see into their world and better understand how they live.

To lay aside myths and uncover truths about snakes.
We fear things that we do not understand. Snakes have been the source of myths and legends since the beginning of our existence. Most of these tales lead us away from the truth. Our fear is born from our lack of knowledge concerning snakes. When we know that a snake means us no intentional harm, fear subsides. We no longer have an urge to destroy them.

To give the reader a basic understanding of venom and snakebites.

When we are aware that a venomous snake is capable of inflicting great bodily harm, even death, we can take steps to minimize that danger. When we are aware that most bites occur when someone tries to catch or kill a snake, we can avoid danger by not trying to catch or kill one. There is nothing I can tell you that can guarantee your safety when in the proximity of a dangerous animal, but hopefully some of this knowledge can decrease your chances of being hurt or killed.

To prepare the reader in case a snake is encountered in the wild.

Again, snakes are fascinating and mysterious creatures. To some, the urge to touch or interact with them is a great temptation. Observing a snake in its natural habitat can be a breath-taking, awe-inspiring experience. The safest thing to do if you encounter a snake is to leave it alone. Observe it from a distance, take pictures, but do not disturb it. Appreciate them, respect them, but do not take chances.

To share basic biological information about the six venomous species native to the Southeastern United States.

Volumes could be written about each of these species, but this is intended to be only an introduction to the dangerous species that someone living within their range may encounter in their own back yards.

In conclusion, my main objective in writing this book is to inform the reader and to hopefully decrease the chances of a snake related accident. Venomous snakebites are extremely painful, potentially deadly, and they are serious medical emergencies. Again, nothing I write can guarantee you won't be snake-bitten, but there are things you can do (or not do!) to decrease those chances. Nothing I write can guarantee that you won't die if bitten, but there are things you can do to decrease those chances. The two most important things I can say to you about snakes are:

• If you see a snake, the safest thing to do is to leave it alone.

• If you are bitten by a snake, get immediate medical attention from a licensed and experienced physician.

Bibliography & Further Reading

**A Field Guide to Reptiles and Amphibians
of Eastern/Central North America,**
Roger Conant

**The Audubon Society Field Guide to
North American Reptiles & Amphibians**
John L. Behler & F. Wayne King

Venomous Reptiles of North America,
Carl H. Ernst, Smithsonian Institution Press

The Venomous Reptiles of the Western Hemisphere,
Jonathan A. Campbell, William W. Lamar, Edmund D. Brodie (Translator)

Rattlesnakes: Their Habits, Life Histories, and Influence on Mankind,
Laurence Monroe Klauber, Karen Harvey McClung

Snake Venom Poisoning,
Findlay E. Russell

Rattlesnake: Portrait of a Predator,
Manny Rubio, William S. Brown

Venomous Snakes: Ecology, Evolution, and Snakebite,
Roger S. Thorpe (Editor), Wolfgang Wuster (Editor), Anita Malhotra (Editor)

http://www.venomousreptiles.org
The Southeastern Hot Herp Society Website

http://treasurecoastwebdesign.com/snakes
Venomous Snakes of Florida by Greg Longhurst

http://www.reptileeducation.com
Southern Reptile Education by B.W. Smith

Chad Minter is a safe, sane, and sober handler of good character who is involved in scientific and educational projects which will contribute significantly to the herpetological community. He has also contributed snakes and field work to venom research.

Tanith Tyrr
Reptile World Serpentarium

Chad has always exhibited the highest degree of respect and responsibility when working with venomous reptiles. He is well versed in the care, handling techniques, and proper caging of venomous reptiles. He is also well educated on the topic of snakebite, and snakebite treatment. He has written articles for the Southeastern Hot Herp Society newsletter which is sent around the world to venomous keepers including Bill Haast, Steve Irwin, Jeff Corwin, and Dean Ripa, world reknowned Bushmaster expert.

Chris Harper, NREMTP
President, Southeastern Hot Herp Society, Inc.

About the Author

Chad Minter has a Bachelors of Science degree in Art Marketing from Georgia College & State University.

He has had a lifelong obsession with venomous reptiles. He has worked for a pet shop, veterinary clinic, wild animal park, and serpentarium. He has literally worked with everything from Aardvarks to Zebras, but his true passion has been with venomous snakes.

He is a former member of the American Society of Icthyologists and Herpetologists, and Former Vice President of the Southeastern Hot Herp Society, Inc., and has authored articles for several publications on safe handling, husbandry, and breeding of venomous reptiles, served on the staff of www.venomousreptiles.org, and appeared in Reptiles Magazine.

He has provided consulting services for the University of Georgia, Boy Scouts of America, Reptile World Serpentarium, Hotlanta Reptiles, U.S. Fish & Wildlife, U.S. Forestry Service, Georgia Department of Natural Resources, The Georgia Herp Atlas Project, General Coffee Gopher Tortoise Survey, Sandy Creek Nature Center, and Chattahoochee Nature Center.

Mr. Minter currently makes his living as a graphic artist, and he is active in the herpetological community. He spends most of his spare time finding and photographing wildlife in its native habitat.

www.ingramcontent.com/pod-product-compliance
Lightning Source LLC
Chambersburg PA
CBHW020355290526
45785CB00005B/2293